IMAGES OF WALES

LLANDUDNO

Llandudno's Coat of Arms reminds us of many chapters in the town's eventful history. The shield shows the ancient St Tudno's church on the Great Orme. Above it are two lions from the arms of the Welsh Princes of Gwynedd (North Wales). In the crest, the Welsh Dragon supports the shield of the Mostyn family, reminding us of the links the town had with this famous family. The hill on which the dragon stands bears two spur-rowels from the arms of the Bishop of Bangor, who had a palace on the hill at Gogarth. The motto *hardd hafan hedd* is the Welsh translation of the phrase 'beautiful haven of peace' an expression attributed to Queen Elizabeth of Roumania during her visit to the town in 1890. Llandudno was granted these fine armorial bearings in 1959.

IMAGES OF WALES

LLANDUDNO

DAVE THOMPSON

TEMPUS

This book is dedicated to Jack Thompson

First published 2005

Tempus Publishing Limited
The Mill, Brimscombe Port,
Stroud, Gloucestershire, GL5 2QG
www.tempus-publishing.com

British Library Cataloguing in Publication Data.
A catalogue record for this book is available from the British Library.

ISBN 0 7524 3683 X
Typesetting and origination by Tempus Publishing Limited.
Printed in Great Britain.

Contents

Acknowledgements

I would like to record my appreciation to the many individuals and organisations who generously provided photographs, shared memories or freely parted with factual material for use in this book. I am indebted to the Imperial War Museum in London, Robbie Buxton, Val Conway, Serena Daroubakhsh, Alvin Forrest, Alan Guinn, David Jones, the late John Jones, Mandy Jones, R.F. Mack, Graham Morgan, Llandudno Town Band, Llandudno Town Council, North Wales Theatre, *North Wales Weekly News*, Paddle Steamer Preservation Society (Scottish Branch), A.D. Packer, R.B. Parr, Judith Phillips, H.B. Priestley, Toby Prosser, Jess Yates estate, and the staff of the Llandudno Library in Mostyn Street for their goodwill and support.

My special thanks are due to George Teare for his work in checking the manuscript and to George H. Brookes MBE (LTB Bandmaster), Jacqueline Millband–Codman, Morris Millband and Dewi Williams for allowing me to make use of their quite unique collections of personal photographs. Without their goodwill and kindness I would not have embarked on the completion of the book.

Introduction

The headland of the Great Orme provides a dramatic backdrop to Llandudno and it is here that much of the town's earliest history is revealed. The Great Orme is an archaeological site of world importance, concealing the largest complex of Bronze Age copper mines found anywhere on earth. Although an inhabited settlement has been in existence for over 4,000 years, this book draws its impressions primarily from the last 150 years.

Llandudno owes its name to St Tudno, who established a monastic cell on the Great Orme in the sixth century and brought Christianity to this wild and desolate part of North Wales. A small hamlet steadily grew on the Orme's south-eastern slopes with inhabitants who, for the most part, found self-sufficiency through fishing, farming and the last vestiges of the ancient mines. For centuries this isolated Welsh-speaking community was insignificant, so much so that Dr Johnson paid it no attention when he reported on his lengthy excursions through North Wales in 1774.

In the 1840s steamboats from Liverpool began ferrying passengers along the North Wales coast and a fledgling number of excursions were made to the village, with visitors brought ashore by rowing boats. Soon even the *Liverpool Mercury* began writing of Llandudno as a fine bathing place. What then occurred was the event which was to shape the town's destiny forever. The Hon. Edward Mostyn MP set forth with a speculative venture to exploit the emerging craze that the middle classes were clearly acquiring for taking the air at summer resorts. With the support of the Bishop of Bangor, Mostyn was able, in 1843, to tease through parliament an Enclosure Act that gave him sole rights to develop the low isthmus between the north and west shores. He commissioned a survey from the Liverpool Architect, Owen Williams, who set forth with imaginative designs for the resort town, shaped with a grid of spacious thoroughfares and a sweeping promenade. Llandudno as we know it was soon to be born.

In 1848 the Apportionment Award parcelled up the area with Mostyn holding a steadfast grip on most of the land. He set about creating his new resort town, although having now dispensed with the services of Williams in favour of a London firm of town planners. Initial interest in developing the barren land below the Great Orme was slow but by 1854 Mostyn Street had taken shape as the main thoroughfare. Soon some of the finest shops outside of London would find a home beneath its wrought iron and glass verandas. The St George's Hotel became the first great hotel to open on the seafront and in 1849 the first landing stages were built, bringing a steadier flow of holidaymakers, particularly those from Liverpool and the other prosperous Lancashire towns.

In the formative years of the late Victorian era many new developments took place to satisfy the swelling number of leisure seekers, these included the construction of the Happy Valley, Llandudno Pier and the Great Orme Tramway. With its temperate climate, fresh breezes and fine setting Llandudno became an elegant resort unrivalled by any other in the principality. Among its distinguished patrons were Napoleon III, Bismarck, Disraeli, Gladstone and the poet Matthew Arnold, who wrote lavish praise of the town. Llandudno was labelled the 'Cambrian Naples' and 'Queen of the Welsh Resorts' – a name which has persisted in marketing material to this day. One of Llandudno's most celebrated visitors was Queen Elizabeth of Roumania, who during her stay in 1890 called the resort a 'beautiful haven of peace.' The reference has literally stayed with Llandudno, her words translated into Welsh now form the town's motto – *hardd, hafan, hedd*.

The town grew considerably throughout the late nineteenth century and into the Edwardian age. New settlers brought with them a close-knit spirit, evident in the plethora of churches, entertainment and social societies being established. Many faiths established churches at Llandudno and many different types of sport and recreation established homes here, including football, rugby and cricket. In 1894 the new Llandudno Town Council was established, to guide the town's prosperity and development as an expanding township. One very obvious change after the First World War was the growth and development of the Craig-y-Don area. By 1921 some 12,900 people lived in the Llandudno area, double what the population had been thirty years earlier.

Llandudno has always managed to remain forever popular with new generations of holidaymakers and unlike many rival resorts on the south and east coasts of England, emerged unscathed from the Second World War. It was quickly able to resume a healthy holiday trade after the war with the first pleasure steamers resuming service in 1946. Before the motor car became the mainstay of family travel the coastal packet steamers played an influential role in Llandudno's development. As many as 3,000 people a day landed at the pier, swelling the coffers of the town's shops, entertainers and hoteliers.

It is hoped that this book has been able to capture the essence of bygone Llandudno. Some pictures were chosen to illustrate significant landmarks, others simply to allow us to glimpse scenes of the town, seen as past generations knew it. Recalled here are the faces of celebrated visitors and citizens, glimpses of events and happenings from Llandudno's past, old modes of transport and cherished street scenes.

Dave Thompson
July 2005

one

Early Llandudno and the Great Orme

This artist's impression from 1852 provides us with a glimpse of how Llandudno looked a few years before Edward Mostyn realised his ambition for the development of a resort town. Across the marshy scrub can be seen nothing but a few scattered cottages on the shoreline. The 1843 Enclosure Act allowed the drainage and parcelling up of the land which resulted in these properties being demolished to make way for the new town.

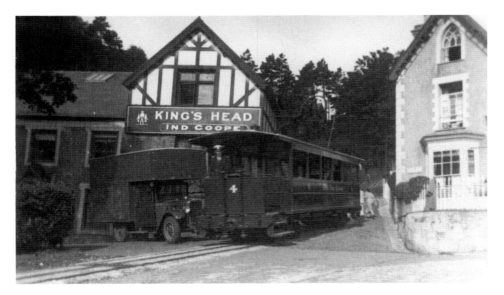

The modern story of Llandudno is etched in the walls of the King's Head. The public house was made famous in 1844 when the Liverpool Architect Owen Williams was heard to say that the area would make an ideal watering place. News of the architect's impressions for a resort reached the ear of Lord Mostyn who immediately seized on the suggestion creating, roughly to Williams' original concept, the layout of the modern town.

Early in the town's fledgling history were plans to export coal and establish a packet boat port to Ireland. As it happens, both time and circumstances intervened. This lithograph engraving from 1854 reveals how the proposed 'Port Wrexham' might well have looked. Note the loading pier on the promenade and the connecting railway line that can be seen passing through Prince Edward Square.

The streets of Llandudno really took shape between the 1850s and 1880s. The grid–pattern streets were planned in parallel to the parade and it was intended that no building should be built higher than the width of the street in which it stood. The results are already evident in this picture postcard view from the turn of the nineteenth century.

In 1872, in the earliest pioneering days of photography, Mr J.J.W. Grainger of Oxford took this fascinating view of Llandudno.

Tramway, Great Orme, Llandudno.

The old copper-mining district on the slopes of the Great Orme. This was a small Welsh-speaking community of 318 inhabitants in 1801 but by the time this picture was taken in 1910 it had grown fourfold in number.

The site of copper-mining activity on the Great Orme has now developed as a tourist attraction. Opened in 1991, the Bronze Age Copper Mines allow visitors the chance to explore 250ft below the surface.

Archaeologists pictured at work on the surface excavations, 1992.

Left: Bone tools and other implements have been unearthed in the six acres of mine-workings, *c.* 1992.

Below: A view of the Great Orme in 1906. The surface of the headland is littered in places with mining spoil and reminders of the past. The ancient mines were known to have been worked again from the sixteenth century until the mid-nineteenth century, when the resort town began to finally take shape.

There was a time when a journey around the Great Orme was an unforgettable experience. Marine Drive was preceded by Cust's Path, an extremely perilous and narrow footway so frightening that in 1868 Prime Minister William Gladstone had to be blindfolded to journey along it. Marine Drive was completed in 1878 at a cost of £14,000 and extends around almost five miles of coastline. This view shows the entrance to the Marine Drive, *c.* 1923.

Toll houses were built at either end of Marine Drive. Among its original charges pedestrians paid 1d, cyclists 2d, saddled horses 3d and carriages 6d per horse. Tolls are still collected today from this toll house and are now payable to Conwy County Borough Council.

Left: A view of 'The Nose' rock, *c.* 1925. This bulbous limestone rock extended over one of the narrowest sections of Marine Drive.

Below: Marine Drive, *c.* 1917.

Coach tours have long provided a quicker and less strenuous means of exploring the Great Orme and services still operate today from Prince Edward Square. These Marine Drive tour buses are pictured by the pier.

The summit complex at the Great Orme has a mixed history. In 1840 it was a telegraph station, part of a series of stations transmitting signals between Holyhead and Liverpool. Later the luxury hotel pictured here was opened, and an 18-hole golf course was added in 1909. The Summit Hotel was requisitioned by the RAF in 1941 for use as a radar station but resumed its former use after the war and was restyled into Randy's Bar and Holiday Centre by Boxer Randolph Turpin, who became co-owner and landlord in 1952.

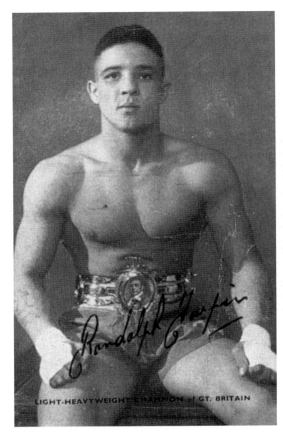

LIGHT-HEAVYWEIGHT CHAMPION of GT. BRITAIN

Left: The name of Randolph Turpin will forever be linked with the summit complex and the bar within the building still bears his name today. The boxer sent shockwaves around the sporting world in 1951 by beating Sugar Ray Robinson to become the world middleweight boxing champion. During his tenure the complex even had an open-air boxing ring where Turpin demonstrated his fighting prowess. These picture postcards were signed and sold as souvenirs from Randy's Bar.

Below: St Tudno's church takes its name from the small monastic community founded here by the Welsh Christian missionary in the sixth century. The ancient church has been rebuilt many times over the centuries before taking the shape that appears in this 1932 picture postcard. It still has some ancient features within it including a splendid twelfth-century font.

ST. TUDNO'S CHURCH, LLANDUDNO.

Open-air Sunday services in the summer are a longstanding tradition of the church, once important for villagers but latterly becoming popular with Christian holidaymakers. The church has an outside pulpit.

Before the development of the town in the 1850s most citizens were buried in St Tudno's ancient churchyard. This was extended early in the twentieth century and an accompanying chapel built. This view from 1920 shows the new burial ground.

The view from the Great Orme offers a dramatic backdrop to the imposing gravestones in the cemetery at St Tudno's church. It has been said that this is one of the few places in Wales where the dead can be considered to rest over the living.

Happy Valley was initiated by Lord Mostyn as part of his original designs for the resort town and was formerly a quarry. It is reputed that troupes of musical entertainers gathered in this vicinity long before it became a formalised outdoor venue in 1887.

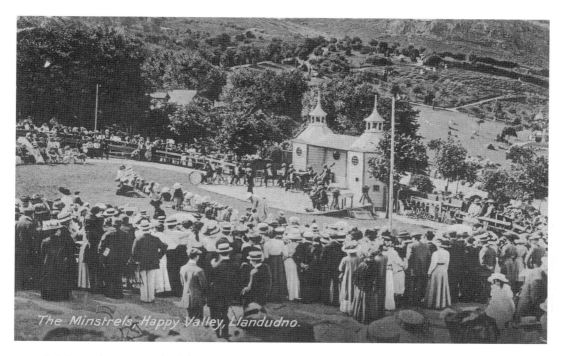

The Minstrels, Happy Valley, Llandudno.

It is interesting to note the fashions on show in this picture, all the women are wearing long pleated dresses and straw hats – clearly the favoured headwear. The wealthier members of the audience invariably hired deckchairs, while many others watched from the hill.

CHURCHILL'S MINSTRELS - HAPPY VALLEY - LLANDUDNO.   Chic Studio

Churchill's Minstrels at Happy Valley were probably the best known performers in the late nineteenth century. Billy Churchill himself was a fine, seasoned entertainer, credited with having performed at the very first Royal Command Performance in 1912.

Charles Wade's Concord Follies enthralled visitors to the open-air theatre in the 1930s. This troupe performed song and dance routines, interspersed with comedy, and they were immensely popular.

This 1937 picture shows Charles Wade's Concord Follies in one of their many stage costumes.

Roy Cowl's Queeries pictured during their 1930 summer season.

The Llandudno Town Band were also regulars on the Happy Valley stage, performing here every Sunday afternoon. This stage picture dates from 1952.

A beautiful summer's day and hardly a blade of grass has not been not claimed by the crowd. Happy Valley was a fine setting for open-air theatre. The only distraction was the occasional steamship, passing to or from the pier.

The Great Orme Cable Lift opened in 1969, offering rides from Camera Hill above the Happy Valley to the summit complex. The two-mile journey provides spectacular views on what is the longest chair lift in the British Isles.

The Happy Valley rock gardens and terraces were reputed to have contained 1,000 species of alpines, rock plants, shrubs and herbaceous plants. It was even claimed that fifty annuals could be found in flower at Christmas.

The rock gardens were laid out by Henry Pochin who later designed the Bodnant Gardens. This fine view dates from around 1927.

Haulfre Gardens was once colourfully described in the following terms, 'A sun trap nestling on the south side of the Orme, offering a charming ensemble of blossom beds, fairy bowers, leafy walks and terraces'. The gardens were opened in 1929 by that most loved of Welshmen, David Lloyd Jones.

Invalids' Walk joins Haulfre Gardens with the West Shore. Alice Liddell, who was the inspiration behind Lewis Carroll's character in *Alice's Adventures in Wonderland*, is said to have regularly used this path as it is close to her childhood home on the West Shore.

two

A stroll along the prom

An aerial view of the promenade in the 1950s. Llandudno's prom is widely recognised as one of the finest in Europe. It extends around almost two miles of seafront and attracts, to its elegant paraded frontages, some of the best hotels and hydros in Wales. At one time it was reputed that Llandudno had more beds for visitors than every other resort in the rest of Wales combined.

Originally known as the Hydropathic and Winter Residence, the Hydro Hotel once provided hydropathic treatments and supposedly health-enhancing therapies. It opened in 1860 and was the realm for many years of Dr Henry Thomas, who was professionally unqualified to practise, yet dispensed hazardous poisons as a remedy for ailments. His cure for diphtheria was a measure of hydrochloric acid in water! Fortunately today's visitors to the Hydro have a more appealing choice on the menu.

On the eastern end of the North Parade – beyond Bodafon Fields – once stood the windswept Craigside Hydro. The luxurious bathing treatments available here included Turkish, Russian, sea-water and plunge baths. The premises closed in 1974.

One of the most historic hotels in the central promenade is the Marine Hotel, pictured here around 1930. It is best recalled as the temporary residence of Queen Elizabeth of Roumania during her five-week stay at Llandudno in 1890.

IMPERIAL HOTEL, LLANDUDNO.

Telephone No. 6.

Telegrams: "Chantrey, Llandudno."

LOUNGE.

PASSENGER LIFT.

ELECTRIC LIGHT IN EVERY ROOM.

NIGHT PORTER.

PRIVATE OMNIBUS.

STABLING.

MOST CENTRALLY SITUATED ON PROMENADE, FACING SEA.   GOLF LINKS.

Illustrated Tariff will be sent on application to

SPECIAL TERMS FOR FAMILIES

JOHN CHANTREY, Proprietor.

Mostyn Crescent contains some of the earliest seafront boarding houses, many of which merged in 1872 to form the Imperial Hotel. This advertisement from around 1901 reminds us just how lavish Llandudno's seafront hotels were, proprietor John Chantrey offered electric lights in every room and even stabling for your horse! Note the telephone number for the hotel is just '6', hardly a number callers could forget.

IMPERIAL HOTEL, & MOSTYN CRESCENT, LLANDUDNO.

A view along the Mostyn Crescent area of the parade, with the Imperial Hotel on the left. The exiled Queen Rambai of Siam resided at the hotel until 1940, when the premises were taken over by the Inland Revenue. Jim Callaghan, who later became Prime Minister, worked at the Imperial for most of the war years and lived a few doors away at No. 7 Mostyn Crescent.

St George's Hotel had the distinction of becoming the town's first seafront hotel in 1855. Not surprisingly many tales in the history of the resort town have their origins within this great hotel. Several Prime Ministers have stayed at the St George's – including Disraeli, Gladstone and more latterly Tony Blair. Llandudno's first omnibus service operated between the hotel and Conwy railway station, before the opening of the town's own railway station.

32603. LLANDUDNO, PROMENADE.

Pre-First World War photographs, such as this early picture postcard, invariably show a line of wheeled wooden sheds along the beachfront. These bathing machines could be hired during the summer months to help spare the blushes of those who sought the 'purifying waters' and to prevent people gazing upon bathers. In 1866 Llandudno beach was served by 137 bathing machines and a few of them were still on the beach in the early 1950s.

This picture dates from the 1890s and provides a clearer impression of the bathing machines. Within the huts bathers changed into beach attire before it was pulled to the water's edge by horse. At the end of

their session, bathers would swim back to their bathing machine and get dressed before signalling to the owner that the hut required pulling back to dry land.

Left: Ladies pose for a photograph beside bathing machine No. 104.

Below: Dr James Nicol, medical officer to the town in the late nineteenth century, went to considerable lengths to justify the town's claims for inducing good health. He made meteorological observations for forty years and proclaimed in a pamphlet that Llandudno had a superior climate to rival resorts on the south coast of England. He professed that this 'Cambrian Naples' received its good share of the genial warmth continuously being imported to North Wales by the Gulf Stream. Dr Nicol said, 'It is indeed astonishing how soon, under the influence of our dry, pure and bracing air, the pallid cheek and pasty complexion are replaced by the hue and glow of health'.

Right: One of the world's oldest theatrical traditions still thrives in Llandudno, more than 140 years after this remarkable man settled here in 1860. Richard Codman (1830-1909) established his Punch and Judy show in the vicinity of Church Walks using glove puppets he had carved out of driftwood from the beach. Codman's show was not thought suitable for the promenade and he faced a four-year struggle with the local powers that be before finally acquiring a permanent prom pitch in 1864. He is pictured here in 1865.

Below: Crowds flocked to view Codman's amazing portrayal of comic tragedy and the power and quality of his performances won him many admirers. During the lean winter months he performed outside Liverpool's Lime Street station and offered short interval acts in theatres at Liverpool and elsewhere. Queen Victoria and many famous celebrities are among those to have viewed his Punch and Judy performances.

Left: This view was probably taken before the First World War and shows the cotton-sided stage at the entrance to the pier. In those early days the proscenium and other staging was once left overnight on the promenade and Codman arrived the morning after a storm to discover his show had been swept out to sea. Undaunted by the setback he secured the services of a diver to recover the framework. Not all the parts were found but thankfully he did recover the stunning hand-carved proscenium.

Below: Following Richard Codman's death in 1909 the seaside traditions of glove puppetry continued in the hands of his youngest son, eighteen-year-old Herbert Codman. He continued Punch and Judy shows on the promenade for the next fifty years, until his own death in 1961. Herbert performed his shows in Welsh or English, depending on the composition of his audiences. This picture, from the 1940s, shows Herbert Codman alongside his canine companion Toby. The Cairn terrier had a valuable role to play in the shows, even biting Punch's nose!

Richard's grandson Jack Codman continued the business in 1961 following a twenty-year apprenticeship under his father. This picture of Jack in the 1970s shows the stunning timber proscenium that was carved by his grandfather over a century earlier.

Overleaf: Pleased as Punch! Young children from the North Wales School for Physically Handicapped Children meet Mr Punch during the 1970s. Jack regularly performed school shows, introducing new generations to the famous characters of Punch and Judy.

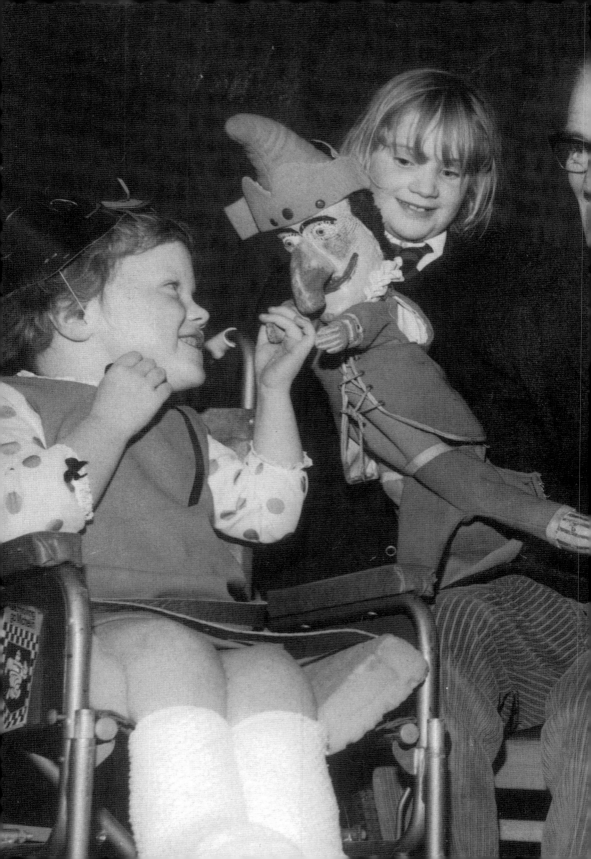

Left: Since 1980 Llandudno's greatest family-run tradition has been in the care of Jack's daughter, Jacqueline Millband and her husband Morris. New generations still thrill to the wooden characters, although Richard's fragile and chipped driftwood puppets have been spared further damage and are now replaced with new dolls.

Below: A crowded beach scene, *c.* 1908. Being beside the seaside was never a straightforward matter in times past. Initially strict rules required separate zones for men and women on the beach and heavy fines befell anyone who dared stray across a 150 yard 'no go zone'. In 1865 byelaws also put paid to bathing naked without an 'apron or drawers', something then common among male bathers.

Sex segregation ended in 1894 allowing families to make better use of the beach. This scene from 1910 reveals a more relaxed atmosphere on the Sands.

One holiday brochure wrote of the Sands in 1933, 'The shore is well adapted for sandcastle building, and a special feature is made of this perennial seaside sport. Competitions are frequently arranged and valuable prizes given for the best sandcastles. Deckchairs may be hired on the Sands, and thousands of visitors may be seen daily drawing strength from the sea breezes in this restful fashion'. This 1926 view shows a sandcastle competition in progress.

Donkey rides have been provided on the Sands from Victorian times but not without a fight. The ruling authorities in the town banned donkeys from the beach but later relented as they had done with Codman's Punch and Judy. This picture postcard scene dates from 1905.

Deckchairs and donkeys are not the only feature of the promenade. Seagulls are all part of the holiday experience, as seen here around 1913.

A view over the Pier Pavilion looking towards Prince Edward Square. The pavilion opened in 1886 and was one of the key attractions of Llandudno. It most famously housed Jules Riviere's Pier Orchestra, conducted under the hand of the indomitable man himself.

The Pier Pavilion Orchestra pose with Jules Riviere standing in the centre. The eccentric conductor was known for many strange traits, not least his novel practice of conducting while facing the audience.

A rare view of the pavilion stage. After its switch to variety most of the leading performers of the day appeared here, including George Formby and Arthur Askey. The Pier Pavilion was also a popular venue for political rallies and its walls once resonated to the sound of Lloyd George, Winston Churchill, Neville Chamberlain and other famous figures. In 1948 a young Margaret Thatcher made her first stage appearance here at the Conservative Party Conference.

THE LLANDUDNO PIER and PAVILION

General Manager and Secretary: T. TURNER PILLING.   Telephone 7140.

SEASON 1933.

SUNDAY, MONDAY, TUESDAY & WEDNESDAY EVENINGS	THURSDAYS AND SATURDAYS	FRIDAY EVENINGS	EVERY DAY
George Cathie AND THE CELEBRATED **Pier Orchestra** WITH THE WORLD'S LEADING ARTISTS	**Dancing** IN THE Spacious Pavilion Ballroom	Grand Symphony **CONCERTS** BY SPECIALLY AUGMENTED ORCHESTRA UNDER THE DIRECTION OF George Cathie	At 11-0 a.m. GEORGE CATHIE AND THE Pier Light Orchestra At 3-0 p.m. GEORGE CATHIE AND THE Pier Bijou Orchestra At 8-0 p.m. (Sundays Excepted) HUGH STANHOPE'S famous "SUMMER SMILES" Concert Party

For Easter Attractions, see our Announcements.

For all that is best in Music and Entertainment—

Visit "THE PEERLESS PIER."

4d. Admission to Morning and Afternoon Concerts and to the Pier at all times of the day **4d.**

Entrance Llandudno

A typical picture postcard view of the pier entrance to the Sands in 1908. Despite the difficulty of photographing busy promenades – with cumbersome cameras and curious onlookers who moved and spoilt the pictures – Llandudno stationers like Taylor's at Gloddaeth Street were able to produce hundreds of different images, sending scenes of Llandudno to all corners of the world.

Opposite below: An advertisement for the 1933 season at the so-called 'peerless pier'. Resident symphony ended at the Pier Pavilion in 1936, after which it switched to a popular mix of repertory and variety performances.

Another picture postcard view of the Pier Pavilion, *c.* 1904. This postcard was destined for Miss Preston at Knott End, near Preston, and the sender remarks, 'This is where we were this Sunday'. In the days before mobile phones, texting and e-mail, picture postcards were the main means of communicating our daily experiences away from home.

The pier entrance once thronged with a fashionable and gaily-dressed crowd, enjoying the many entertainments found in the vicinity. The self-proclaimed postcard king, George Thompson, had a kiosk here selling images of the town, some of which have finally made it back into print with the publication of this book.

The viewing of steamships coming and going was a popular pastime for pier strollers. This view dates from 1914.

The end of pier show. The first pier head bandstand is pictured here around 1880. The pier head orchestra offered that unique combination – great sounds and sea air!

This picture postcard from 1908 shows the new larger pavilion that was built on the pier head.

For over twenty years promenade crowds flocked around a makeshift trestle table near the pier entrance. They were drawn by Signor Giciano Ferrari and his amazing performing birds. Ferrari's feathered friends enthralled spectators with a variety of tricks, mostly performed with the aid of accompanying circus props. The entertainer is seen pictured here in 1911.

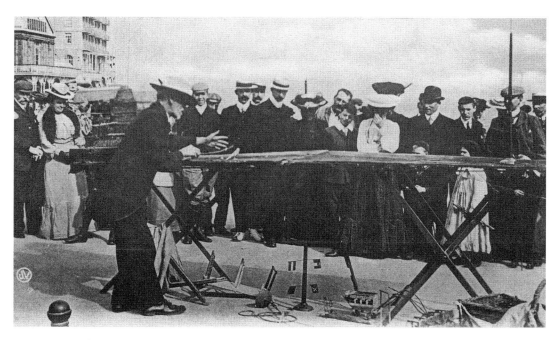

A scene from around 1909 with Ferrari commanding his birds to perform. He even had a cockatoo that flew around the Grand Hotel and returned upon call. Note the many circus props under his makeshift staging area.

'Llandudno is more stylish than either Rhyl or Blackpool, and not dearer', claimed social chronicler Arnold Bennett in his 1911 novel *The Card*. Many of these visitors might well have agreed. Llandudno has always enjoyed a loyal number of visitors who return to the resort year after year.

In Victorian times the promenade had a movable bandstand. Known as 'the juggernaut' this hefty structure could be pulled to its required location. Later, in 1920, this permanent fixed bandstand was

constructed on the promenade. This view from the 1950s illustrates the popularity of summer prom performances by the Llandudno Town Band.

Above: The official opening of the new colonnade in 1932, guests begin to gather before the ceremony gets under way. Just in view to the right is the entrance to the Grand Hotel.

Left: Few seafront hotels have a grander setting than the appropriately named Grand Hotel. Opened in 1901 the hotel was built on the site of the earlier Baths Hotel. In earlier times the Grand was the largest hotel in Wales and its register read like a copy of *Who's Who* with Winston Churchill among an impressive list of past guests. The Grand was used in the 1951 film *The Card* staring Sir Alec Guinness.

Visitors have always been lured by the appeal of seagulls and these promenade strollers at Craig-y-Don in 1933 are no exception.

Craig-y-don Promenade, Llandudno

A picture postcard view along the parade at Craig-y-Don.

The Little Orme, *c.* 1913.

Llandudno once had a short-lived shipbuilding industry which centred on the West Shore. Ironically it later became known to the Edwardians as a popular place for the sailing of miniature model yachts.

Model yachtsmen came from all parts of Britain to compete in the sailing races organised by the Town Improvement Association, sometimes large crowds viewed the races as can be seen in this 1933 photograph. Rule cards were obtainable from the Town Hall and yachts 'warranted to sail' could be bought at local shops. Also seen in the background are the Gogarth Abbey Hotel and the white miners' cottages built in 1783 during a short revival in the fortunes of the copper industry.

There is still something magical about the West Shore. The Liddell family, of *Alice's Adventures in Wonderland* fame, loved the splendour of this place and built a home here. The fine panoramic views of the Conwy estuary, Penmaenmawr mountains and Anglesey are said to have inspired Lewis Carroll to write *Alice's Adventures in Wonderland* in 1866, but evidence to support this claim has never come to light. This view of the West Shore was taken in the 1930s.

Above: The West Shore viewed from the lower slopes of the Great Orme. The shore was gifted in 1284 from King Edward to the Bishop of Bangor in appreciation of his christening of the first English Prince of Wales.

Left: The Victorian political reformer John Bright was an enthusiastic patron of Llandudno. In one speech he said of the town, 'When I look at the position of your town on the beautiful bay, when I look around me and see the beauties of your locality, when I remember how near you are to the finest scenery of this glorious Wales, when I observe and enjoy the purity of your climate, when I remember all the courtesy and all the kind attention with which I have met, I am free to say that I have great faith in your future'.

three

The streets of town

The curving grid pattern of Llandudno's streets have taken shape, as seen in this 1904 picture postcard. The streets and thoroughfares of the resort town had been sketched out in the 1850s, but look carefully and you will note that the Craig-y-Don district had not yet been developed.

GENERAL VIEW LLANDUDNO

This 1913 picture postcard view was probably taken from Invalids' Walk. It shows a sea of rooftops and chimneys where less than a century earlier there had been marshland and scrub. Llandudno's population by this time had reached almost 11,000 – ten times the number that had existed when the resort town was conceived sixty years earlier.

Church Walks is one of Llandudno's most historic roads. It is named after St George's church and some of the town's best known personalities including Jules Riviere, the eccentric conductor of the Pier Pavilion orchestra, resided there.

Another view of Church Walks taken in the early 1920s before motor cars began dominating the street scene. Many prominent buildings were built on Church Walks including the Empire Hotel which can be seen to the left in this view.

Taken from outside the Queens Hotel, a horse-drawn carriage passes along the parade. The carriage is probably a tour coach, which were popular when this image was taken at the end of the nineteenth century. Bathing machines can also be viewed on the beach.

The same view in the 1930s. Note the appearance of cars along the parade. A decision has also now been taken to remove trees (as seen in the above photograph) from along the seafront.

The curving frontages of hotels on the North Parade remain the most symbolic statement of Llandudno's classical elegance, 1908.

Prince Edward Square is hardly square at all. Within this triangular area of the North Shore are fifty-one listed buildings, demonstrating the architectural significance of this locality. At the time this picture was taken in 1908 the cenotaph had not been erected and there is no problem with finding car parking spaces! This view looks exactly how the town planners had first envisaged it.

Left: The war memorial was erected on the North Parade in 1922 offering a highly prominent expression of the town's grief at the loss of so many men on the battlefields of Flanders and France. The emblem of the Royal Welch Fusiliers adorns the top of the obelisk.

Below: Laid out in the 1850s, Mostyn Street has always been the principal shopping street in Llandudno. In Victorian times the wrought-iron and glass veranda frontages concealed some of the most exclusive shops in Wales, patronised in many cases by the titled guests who stayed in the classy seafront hotels. It was even said that Mostyn Street had more royal warrants than any shopping street outside of London. This view dates from 1911.

MOSTYN STREET, LLANDUDNO.

Right: The triangular area of land which stands at the junction of Vaughan Street and Mostyn Street is one of Llandudno's most historic open spaces. North Western Gardens was used as a private hotel garden until 1902 when Llandudno Urban District Council bought the land for a public park. This view was taken from the North Western Hotel, one of the two hotels which overlooked the gardens.

NORTH WESTERN GARDENS and
MOSTYN STREET, LLANDUDNO.

Below: Another early view of the gardens showing people relaxing in the park.

NORTH-WESTERN HOTEL.

Conveniently Situated.

❁

Three Minutes' from Centre of Bay.

Refurnished and Redecorated.

❁

Electric Light Throughout.

TABLE D'HÔTE 6-30 P.M.

Telephone No. 68.   Entirely under New Management.   *Miss CURRIE, Manageress.*

An advertisement for the North Western Hotel from the beginning of the twentieth century. It shows a leisurely game of croquet being enjoyed in the town centre, hardly something one would expect today! The hotel later became known as the Tudno Castle Hotel and is today known simply as the Castle Hotel.

Excellent shops and a superb mix of fresh produce and goods were the hallmark of this area of Mostyn Street. George Thompson, the so-called 'postcard king' had a shop opposite North West Gardens. Many of the fine views shown in this book were taken by the printer and stationer.

This lovely picture postcard view of Mostyn Street from 1917 shows horse-drawn carts still holding sway on the streets as late as the First World War.

A street scene looking towards the Church of Wales, Holy Trinity church at Trinity Square, *c.* 1953.

Charlton Street from Fildes Hotel, Llandudno.

A rare view along Charlton Street in the direction of Holy Trinity church. The street is named after Sir John Charlton the former Chairman of the Great Orme's Marine Drive Co.

How many town centres can boast such a dramatic backdrop as the one the Great Orme affords Mostyn Street? The 679ft southern slopes of the Great Orme tower over the upper section of Mostyn Street.

The view along Mostyn Street in the opposite direction.

An advertisement for Roberts & Sons fishmongers, one of the oldest shops trading in Llandudno in 1933. Like many other traders in the town, they proudly boasted of Queen Elizabeth of Roumania having once been a customer, hence its somewhat far-fetched description as 'The Royal Fish Stores'.

A cold winter's day seems evident in this picture. Note the icy pavements in Mostyn Street. St John's Methodist church can be seen to the right. It opened in 1866, pioneering Methodism in the town.

Gloddaeth Avenue was completed as an extension of Gloddaeth Street. Many fine buildings can be found on this impressive thoroughfare, such as the Presbyterian church which can be seen to the left in this Edwardian picture postcard view. The church was built in 1905.

A busy scene in Gloddaeth Street, *c.* 1953.

Side by side. By the time this photograph was taken in 1953 the motor car was finally surpassing the tram in the everyday street scene.

Above: The Llandudno tram was unique in its day. A varied assortment of electric trams saw service on the streets, operating between Llandudno and stops along the way to Colwyn Bay. In 1956 the managing company switched to motorbuses but struggled to compete against Crosville and ceased trading in 1961.

Left: Boarding establishments were plentiful along the main streets of Edwardian Llandudno, swelling the population for much of the year. Gloddaeth Avenue and other thoroughfares were bordered with many lofty lodging houses like Tynedale, pictured here on Lloyd Street.

Left: This picture postcard dates from a time when Llandudno had nearly thirty places of worship. As the old copper village prospered and tourism flourished, many faiths established a foothold in the community and by 1891 there was one church or chapel for every 366 residents. Under the influence of Revd Richard Parry, Christ Church, off Abbey Road, actively promoted services in English. However, the modern-day fortunes of this once-beautiful church have not been so good, part of its spire has been removed and it is no longer in use for church services.

Below: Craig-y-Don means 'the rock by the waves'. The district became a popular residential area after the First World War when many spacious roads were constructed, most with names that reflected the town's history.

CRAIG-Y-DON & GREAT ORME, LLANDUDNO.

This picture postcard from 1925 shows how the Craig-y-Don district had quickly developed between the town centre and Bodafon Fields.

Mostyn Avenue, c. 1950. To the left is St Paul's church which was built as a memorial to the Duke of Clarence. Pointing to wholly circumstantial evidence, amateur sleuths have repeatedly suggested that the Duke was none other than Jack the Ripper, the infamous Victorian killer from London's Whitechapel district.

Another Mostyn Avenue view, this time looking northwards.

This is an early view of Carmen Sylva Road. The road was named after the pseudonym used by Queen Elizabeth of Roumania, who was a novelist and penned romantic works.

Queens Road is arguably the best known thoroughfare at Craig-y-Don since it leads in and out of town. The road is named after Queen Victoria, as is the local park.

Queens Park at Craig-y-Don.

four

People's century

The social goings-on at Llandudno are captured in this chapter. Someone certain to have known more than most about these events would have been the local Town Crier. This rare undated picture shows the luggage cart of Llandudno's one time Town Crier. The small lettering on the cart suggests this man is Mr Roberts, Town Crier of Pengwern Cottage, North Parade.

The Oval Cricket Ground off Gloddaeth Avenue has been used since 1891 and many first-class matches have been played here including Wales' performances against New Zealand and the West Indies in the 1920s. This picture shows Wales in action against Ireland in 1925.

The best days of their lives. Schoolchildren at Lloyd Street school pose for a class picture in 1929. Many of the children are dressed in costume ready for their end of year play at the Grand Theatre.

A class of seniors from John Bright school, 1934.

This picture from 1952 shows the Arcadia theatre, one of Llandudno's best known entertainment venues. It opened as the Victoria Palace in 1894 and had several name changes before its owners settled on the identity for which it was best known. The Arcadia was intended to have been the first phase in the construction of a second pier but the development never emerged. In the foreground of this picture workmen can be seen undertaking essential maintenance to the tramlines at Craig-y-Don.

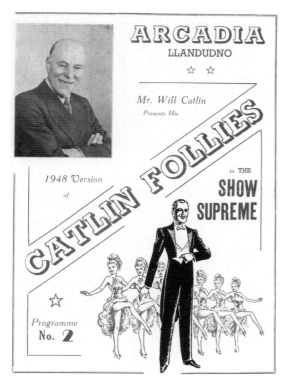

This 1948 programme details the entertainment provided at the Arcadia by Mr Will Catlin. His 'Catlin Follies' played to packed houses for many years. The impresario collapsed and died on the promenade in 1953.

Above: The Odeon on Gloddaeth Street was a huge monolithic entertainment complex, offering various forms of entertainment including theatre, cinema, opera and dances. It was originally known as the Winter Gardens and is pictured here in 1947. Billy Connolly was the last person to perform at the Odeon in 1986.

Left: An advertisement for Llandudno's Grand Theatre. The magnificent 1,000-seat venue staged some of the best touring productions, but is best known for BBC entertainment broadcasts during the Second World War. The Grand Theatre is now a nightclub better suited to the needs of the town's more rumbustious fun seekers.

The Llandudno Town Band has provided the musical beat of Llandudno's heart for almost a century. It was constituted by the Urban District Council in 1910 but has its origins earlier in the 1880s when the Tudno Silver Band was assembled. This picture was taken outside the Pier Pavilion.

The band entertained holidaymakers every night of the summer season on their promenade bandstand and offered Sunday afternoon concerts at the Happy Valley. This 1921 picture sees them posed just before band practice gets underway.

Left: The success of the Llandudno Town Band was a tribute to the endeavours of its fine conductor, F. Lucio Traversi. The cornet playing New Zealander led the band from its inception in 1910 and conducted it until his retirement in 1948.

Below: Unlike many concert bands the Llandudno Town Band kept playing during the war years, and there probably has not been an important public occasion since when they have not performed. Mr Traversi overcame the problem of band players being drafted into war service by establishing a learner's class. Within a couple of years some of the boys, pictured here in 1940, were performing nightly throughout the Second World War.

The Llandudno Town Band leads the uniformed and voluntary services along Mostyn Street, *c.* 1942.

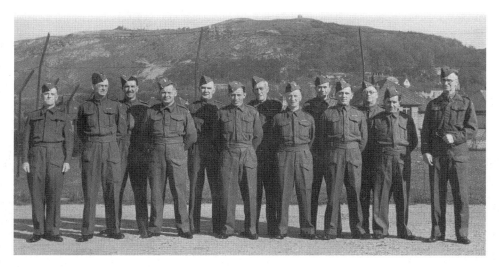

Llandudno's own Dad's Army defenders. The Home Guard organised the civil defence of the town during the war years. Some of the men had previously served their country during the First World War and they came from many walks of life. Llandudno's Punch and Judy puppeteer Herbert Codman is among this platoon.

Since its royal gala opening in the presence of Prince Charles in 1994, the 1,505-seat North Wales Theatre has established itself as one of the UK's top provincial theatres. Most forms of live entertainment are performed here, including the staging of top West End shows.

Carnivals and parades have long formed an important part of Llandudno's early social traditions. The crowning of the town's May Queen was one important tradition, rigorously supported for many decades. This photograph from the early 1950s shows May Queen Olga Jones, surrounded by attendants, as she joins the procession to Prince Edward Square.

Today May Day festivities manifest themselves in the form of the annual Victorian Extravaganza. This event is held over the May bank holiday and is one of the busiest weekends of the year. Mostyn Street remains closed as funfairs, street entertainment and steam engines take centre stage.

five

All at sea

There was a time when sailing boats could be hired from the promenade and their canvas sails dominated the scenes across the beach. These boats were heavily regulated by the town's Improvement Commissioners to ensure they were seaworthy and in good repair.

Rowing boats at the jetty, *c.* 1910.

Pleasure trips around the bay have long been popular with summer visitors. Moored at the jetty in this view is the popular pleasure cruiser *White Heather*.

A stormy seafront at Llandudno. The sea has cast a powerful influence on the history of Llandudno. Many of the earliest inhabitants of the area made their livelihood from fishing and more recent generations have benefited from the social prosperity brought about by the coastal pleasure steamers.

This early picture postcard shows Llandudno after a storm has settled. Many small sailing boats can be seen washed up on the beach.

Rough seas and ferocious weather have often had a devastating impact on shipping. For centuries ships foundered along the coastline of the Orme's heads and this only worsened as coastal shipping reached its peak in the 1850s. This topsail schooner is pictured wrecked in the bay during the 1880s.

As a result of the increase in Irish Sea traffic and the worrying regularity of shipwrecks off Llandudno, the Mersey Docks & Harbour Board lessened the risk to shipping when it built a lighthouse on the rocky headland of the Great Orme in 1862. This particular view of the lighthouse is from 1919.

The RNLI established a lifeboat service at Llandudno in 1861. Its first coxswain was a copper miner on the Great Orme and his daughter reputedly rushed to the mineshaft to alert her father whenever a distress call was given. The first lifeboat was a relatively unstable ten-oar rowing boat named *Seven Sisters* and her first active rescue saved the crew of a distressed Runcorn flat *Uncle Tom*. Many other lifeboats subsequently saw service, one of the best known being the *Thomas & Annie Wade Richards*. Between 1933 and 1953 this boat was launched fifty-seven times and rescued thirty-eight people, six of them even before her official launch date. By the time of the Llandudno lifeboat's centenary in 1961 there had been 167 lifeboat launches, rescuing 163 people, many from almost certain death. This dramatic picture shows crowds watching on as the lifeboat *Theodore Price* is launched at the promenade.

'For those in peril on the sea'. The lifeboat *Theodore Price* takes to the waves.

The *Theodore Price* being launched in calmer seas. This twelve-oar, self righting lifeboat saw service between 1902 and 1930 and had the distinction of being partially designed by members of her crew. *Theodore Price* launched forty-two times rescuing thirty-nine people.

Another crowd scene on the promenade, *c.* 1905.

The Llandudno lifeboat has continued to play an active role in the life of the local community and the dedication of a new boat has always been an important occasion. This crowd is assembled on the promenade for the official launch of a new boat in the 1960s.

The presence of the lifeboat continues to draw attention on the promenade. The current Mersey-class boat *Andy Pearce* is pictured here with its submersible tractor. Built in 1990 the 16-knot lifeboat has a range of 140 miles.

No account of Llandudno's ties to the sea would be complete without mention of the pleasure steamers that brought day trippers and holidaymakers to the town from the earliest days of the area's reshaping into a Victorian resort. The Liverpool & North Wales Steamship Co. dominated passenger services. Popular excursions included Anglesey on the *St Trillio*, Douglas on the *St Seriol* and Menai most commonly on the *St Tudno* as an extension of her Liverpool service. One of the earliest and best loved ships in Llandudno's history was the paddle steamer *La Marguerite*. This view shows the historic steamer at sea in 1911.

S. S. La Marguerite, Llandudno.

The *La Marguerite* approaches Llandudno pier. The paddle steamer was built to serve the continental route from Tilbury to Boulogne and was the first steamer capable of doing the cross-channel journey in a day, but was never able to make a profit. As a consequence she was sold in 1904 to the Liverpool & North Wales Steamship Co. for use on their Liverpool, Llandudno and Menai Bridge routes.

The 1,554-ton *La Marguerite* was the most modern steamer of her era and was an instant success, bringing large numbers of passengers to and from Llandudno. She is seen here about to discharge her cargo of happy holidaymakers and day trippers.

The Pier from Great Orme, Llandudno.

La Marguerite seen on her approach to the pier. With the exception of short periods when she had been chartered to the Isle of Man or requisitioned as a troop ship, the *La Marguerite* had continuously serviced the Liverpool, Llandudno and Menai Bridge route for over twenty years. Her final departure from Llandudno in 1925 met with a great deal of emotion and a crowd of many thousands gathered to bid a fond farewell to a ship that had been so influential in the town's prosperity.

The paddle steamer *Snowdon* was originally operated at Llandudno by a small independent firm but was taken over by the Liverpool & North Wales Steam Ship Co. in 1899. *Snowdon* carried 450 passengers and continued in service until 1931.

Full steam ahead. *Snowdon* is seen in a picture postcard from 1912.

The resplendent steamer *St Elvies* was another ship which brought passengers to Llandudno. She was in service until the 1930s.

SAILINGS FROM LLANDUDNO

CONNECTIONS BY TRAIN, ELECTRIC CAR OR MOTOR BUS

By "ST. TUDNO" or "ST. SEIRIOL"

(Weather and other circumstances permitting)

SUBJECT TO ALTERATION WITHOUT NOTICE AND TO CONDITIONS OF CARRIAGE

DAILY, 1.15 p.m. to **MENAI BRIDGE** Return Fare 5/-	**"ST. TUDNO" or "ST. SEIRIOL"** DAILY leaves LIVERPOOL at 10.45 a.m. *Leaves* LLANDUDNO 1.15 p.m. | *Leaves* Menai Bridge ... 3.45 p.m. *Due* Menai Bridge ... 2.35 ,, | *Due* LLANDUDNO ... 5.0 ,, Leaves Llandudno at 5.15 p.m., due Liverpool at 7.30 p.m.
DAILY, 1.15 p.m. **CIRCULAR TOUR** Return Rail 8/- Return Bus 6/- (Children 3/6) (Sundays excepted)	**LLANDUDNO AND MENAI BRIDGE** Passengers travel outward by Steamer (as above) and Return from Menai Bridge (Post Office Square) by any Crosville Service Bus, or by any Train from Menai Bridge Station.
SUNDAYS Fare 5/-	**Grand Anglesey Coast Cruise "ST. SEIRIOL"** Passing PUFFIN ISLAND, RED WHARF AND MOELFRE BAYS **Towards POINT LYNAS** *Leaves* LLANDUDNO ... 1.45 p.m. | *Due back* LLANDUDNO ... 4.45 p.m.
EVERY TUESDAY also **WEDS.** Commencing 4th JULY Day Return 15/-	**DOUGLAS (Isle of Man)** "ST. SEIRIOL" *Leaves* LLANDUDNO 10.15 a.m. | *Leaves* Douglas ... ... 4.30 p.m. *Due* Douglas ... ... 1.30 p.m. | *Due* LLANDUDNO ... 7.50 ,, Corporation Bus Tour from Peveril Square—Tickets from Purser 1/6
WEDNESDAYS 13th and 20th June	("ST. SEIRIOL") **LIVERPOOL** (2 hours ashore) *Leaves* LLANDUDNO 9.30 a.m. | *Leaves* Liverpool ... ... 2.0 p.m. *Due* Liverpool ... 11.50 a.m. | *Due* LLANDUDNO ... 4.20 ,,
CIRCULAR TOUR Return Rail 8/- Return Bus 6/- (Children 3/6) (Sundays excepted)	**MENAI BRIDGE AND LLANDUDNO** Steamer leaves Menai Bridge 3.45 p.m., due Llandudno 5.0 p.m. Passengers return by any Crosville Service Bus, or by any Train from Llandudno Station. Tickets obtainable from Pier Gates Office, Menai Bridge.
BOAT AND RAIL	Through bookings in connection with the above Sailings are in operation from Prestatyn, Rhyl, Abergele, Old Colwyn, Colwyn Bay, Llandudno Junction, Llanfairfechan, Penmaenmawr and Bangor.

FARES (Including Pier Dues)	SINGLE JOURNEY	DAY RETURN Available Day of issue only.	PERIOD RETURN Available until end of Season
Llandudno to **Menai Bridge**	4/-	5/-	
Llandudno to **Liverpool** ...	8/6	7/6	12/6
Llandudno to **Douglas** ...	10/-	15/-	
Menai Bridge to Liverpool	10/-		15/-

CHILDREN OVER 3 AND UNDER 14 YEARS HALF FARE.

REDUCTION FOR PARTIES OF 8 OR MORE IF PREVIOUSLY ARRANGED. PRIVATE CABINS may be Booked in Advance

Holiday Contracts (6 Consecutive Weekdays) 21 /- (Pier Tolls excluded) issued from any date and available all advertised sailings

ALL TICKETS ARE ISSUED, PASSENGERS AND GOODS CARRIED SUBJECT TO THE COMPANY'S CONDITIONS OF CARRIAGE, AS EXHIBITED AT THE COMPANY'S OFFICES AND ON THE VESSELS.

CATERING, LUNCH AND TEAS, BUFFETS AND REFRESHMENT BARS.

For all further particulars apply to the Company's Representative, W. O. Williams, Pier Gates, Llandudno (Tel. 6837); Crosville Motor Services, Colwyn Bay (Tel. 2330); S. A. Roberts, Amity House, Abergele; Crosville Motor Services, Rhyl (Tel. 437); Messrs. Pickfords, Colwyn Bay (Tel. 2852); G. M. Evans, Medical Hall, Church Street, Beaumaris (Tel. 39); Crosville Motor Services Ltd., Bangor (Tel. 148); T. Roberts, 65 Garth Road, Bangor; Menai Bridge Pier (Tel. 12); Messrs. Fritchard Bros., Porth-yr-Aur, Caernarvon (Tel. 219); H. Mathias, 24 Stanley Street, Holyhead; Railway Stations; or to The Liverpool and North Wales S.S. Co. Ltd., 40 Chapel Street, Liverpool (Tel. CENtral 1653/4—Telegrams "ST. TUDNO," Liverpool.

Official Guide 6d.

TICKETS AT COMPANY'S OFFICE, PIER GATES OR FROM AGENTS

For particulars of sailings per M.V. "ST. TRILLO" see other bills

13 (2)

This advertising bill from the early 1960s shows the trips available from Llandudno.

In 1936 the Liverpool & North Wales Steam Ship Co. replaced several of its older Llandudno pleasure cruisers with a diesel engine ship called *St Silio*. She was requisitioned as a troop carrier in 1939 and subsequently renamed *St Trillio* on her return to service at Llandudno in 1946. This 314-ton vessel was capable of carrying 568 passengers, helping to swell the town's post-war popularity for day trippers and holidaymakers for many years to come. The *St Trillio* is pictured here in 1962 when she was being sold to P&A Campbell. Her sister ships were scrapped but Campbell's managed to keep the *St Trillio* in service until 1969.

Luxury hit new heights in 1926 when the pleasure steamer *St Tudno* began service. The 329ft vessel had dining rooms, lounge areas and even a ship's barber. *St Tudno* worked every day from Liverpool to Llandudno and for a period continued on to Menai Bridge.

St Tudno made her last voyage to Llandudno in August 1962. This rare picture taken shortly afterwards shows the famous ship being towed on her way to the breaker's yard.

Ships have not just sailed to and from the town, Llandudno itself even sailed the seas. This is HMS *Llandudno*, the 656-ton Bangor-class minesweeper built in 1941 by William Hamilton & Co. at Port Glasgow. She was capable of 16 knots and had a crew of sixty men. HMS *Llandudno* had a relatively short service life, serving most of the war in Iceland and the south coast of England before being sold by the navy in 1947. (Courtesy of the Imperial War Museum, London, FL 14686)

six

Llandudno
trams

Above: For more than a century the Great Orme Tramway has been one of the most appealing features of Llandudno Bay. The development of tourism combined with the growing potential for housing on the steep gradients of the Great Orme resulted in the Great Orme Tramway Act in 1898. Local businessmen and prominent residents promoted the scheme and spent two years acquiring the necessary land before construction work commenced in 1901. This picture shows Victoria station, the lower terminus from which most journeys commence. From here trams climbed to Black Gate or on to the summit of the Great Orme.

Left: A selection of tram tickets issued between 1951 and the early '70s. Local residents were offered cheaper fares, introduced originally as a means of encouraging residential development. The Great Orme Tramway was also required under the original Act to carry coffins in 'a decent and seemly manner' for interment at St Tudno's churchyard.

Right: A view of the steep lower section of the tramway at Old Road, 1957.

Below: Tram No. 5 is hauled up the tramway's lower section in 1910. This is one of four operational trams that were used on the tramway. This particular tram was fitted with water tanks to allow the driver to use water as a lubricant on the steep and curved lower sections.

34096 LLANDUDNO: TRAMWAY, GREAT ORME.

More than forty years later and tram No. 5 is still passing to and fro on the historic 3ft 6in-gauge tramway. This picture was taken in 1953.

A 1953 view of the tram storage sheds at the halfway station. The tram cables were originally powered by coal-fired steam engines which meant all the coal had to be transported up the Great Orme. The tramway converted to electric haulage in 1958.

Trams No. 6 and No.7 pass each other at the midway point of the upper section in 1958. The rail points here were tripped by the trams passing over them; this avoided collisions and ensured the trams following their respective cables. As well as seeing each other, passengers here also got to see one of the most stunning views enjoyed by tram journey.

Tram No.7 ascends the final stages to the summit in 1952. The tramway has had an eventful history. In 1917 a severe storm actually managed to lift a tram off its tracks at the summit, and in 1932 Llandudno was shaken by tragedy when tram No. 4 crashed killing the driver and a twelve-year-old passenger.

Another packed former Bournemouth tram passes along Mostyn Street. Looking carefully at the road you can see the double tracks that allowed trams to pass each other near Marks & Spencer.

Opposite above: Although Llandudno is renowned for the Great Orme Tramway, equally well known at one time were its street tramcars. The Llandudno & Colwyn Bay Electric Railway (LCBER) began operating tramway services in 1907 providing one of the few 'inter–urban' tramways ever built in Britain. The LCBER operated to and from Colwyn Bay starting from a terminus on the West Shore, before passing down Gloddaeth Avenue, en route to Mostyn Street, where the tramway then headed out of town en route for the Little Orme and other stops.

Opposite below: Over the years many second-hand cars from other municipal services were purchased. The former trams of Accrington, Bournemouth and Darwen were added to services at Llandudno. This view from 1952 shows two ex-Bournemouth cars passing on the corner of Mostyn Street and Gloddaeth Street. These were among a batch of ten cars brought into service in 1936.

Tram No. 21 passing Marks & Spencer in 1954.

Two trams are pictured passing Payne's Corner in the 1950s.

At peak times Hooson's Corner was so busy it often seemed like the terminus for trams to Colwyn Bay.

This single deck bogie car was built in 1915 and bought from Accrington Corporation in 1933. It remained in service at Llandudno until the closure of the tramways in 1956.

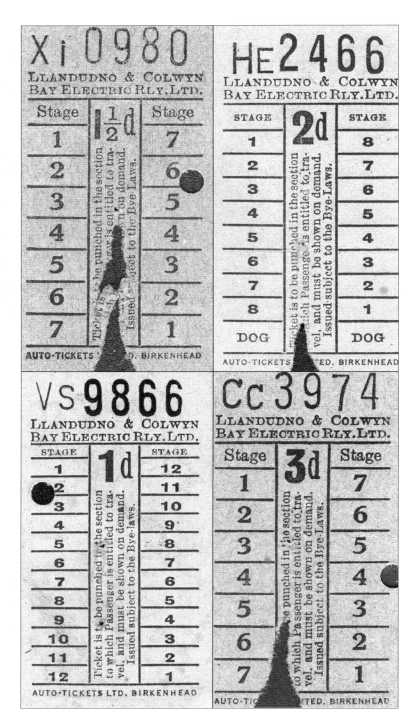

These classic bell-punch tickets were issued to passengers. The lowest fare in 1952 was 1d. Many local shops including Clare's Department Store on Mostyn Street were advertised on the reverse side of the tickets.

The so-called 'toastrack' trams were extremely popular with summer holidaymakers. These sixty-seat open-topped single-deck cars came into service in 1920 and continued in use until tram services were discontinued in 1956.

In downtown Llandudno motorists had to be careful where they parked, lest their car bumper got in the way of a passing tram! Car No. 20 is seen here passing along Gloddaeth Avenue in 1952.

Sporting a slightly misleading destination of 'Llandudno Pier' this toastrack car is destined for
Colwyn Bay; let's hope it did not start raining en route!

A toastrack tram passes Craigside Stop on its way into town. One of the joys of the old toastrack
was that passengers could sit at the front alongside the driver, and these schoolboys doubtless have
fond memories of the excitement they experienced when travelling around in open-topped trams.
Llandudno's tramways lingered on well into the 1950s when most other tramways had closed, but
in 1956 they too finally passed into history. It is reputed the Llandudno trams provided
130 million passenger journeys during their lifetime.

For over a century the castellated shape of the Summit Hotel (at first known as the Telegraph Hotel) greeted visitors who made the worthwhile journey to the summit of the Great Orme. The building has a chequered history but is perhaps best remembered for the nine years it was managed by boxer Randolph Turpin. Since 1965 radio masts have proved a rather unsightly scar on the modernised building.

HAPPY VALLEY MINSTRELS, LLANDUDNO.

The Happy Valley pavilion is one of the most-photographed buildings of old Llandudno and it has provided centre stage for the town's musical traditions for over a century. Originally canvas tents were used in the valley but as crowds swelled a more fixed platform was required. This particular view dates from the 1920s, showing the structure that burnt down in 1933.

Overlooking the sea at Happy Valley is the Queen Victoria Memorial, Llandudno's own tribute to the great monarch who ruled through the first half century after the town's remodelling as a resort. This Edwardian picture postcard illustrates the area's popularity with walkers and leisure seekers.

Lighthouse, Keeper, Coastguard.   Gt. Orme's Head, 325 Ft. above the Sea.

No landmark in Llandudno has made its presence felt more than the Great Orme lighthouse. Perched 370ft above the wave-lashed cliffs of the headland, the lighthouse's 18,500 candlepower lamp could, in the right conditions, be viewed from Snaefell on the Isle of Man.

One Llandudno landmark has the distinction of helping the visitor view local landmarks. The Camera Obscura offers a spectacular elevated view over the town from Camera Hill. Originally built in 1860, the Camera Obscura works by reflecting mirrored images from a rooftop lens, down onto a circular turntable within the darkened room. It closed in 1964 and the original building was later destroyed by fire but this new Camera Obscura has since been rebuilt.

Holy Trinity church is the most commanding church in the centre of Llandudno, standing in its own square between Mostyn Street and Madoc Street. It was built in 1874 to the designs of Lord Mostyn's agent. The church has a stained-glass window dedicated to St Tudno, the patron saint of Llandudno. Its war memorial chapel houses the colours of the 13th and 17th Battalions of the Royal Welch Fusiliers.

The Tabernacle Welsh Baptist chapel on Upper Mostyn Street was originally founded in 1813 and this fine building was built on its site in 1876. A former Minister of the chapel was Revd Lewis Valentine, one of the founders of the Welsh Nationalist Party – Plaid Cymru.

In the decades that they stood together the Pier Pavilion and Grand Hotel cast a domineering and lofty presence across the bay. The Grand Hotel still stands but the Pier Pavilion endured an unfortunate demise at the hands of an arsonist in 1994. This picture postcard view was taken in 1906.

Llandudno Pier remains the supreme expression of the town's ornate Victoriana. Although partially destroyed by fire in 1994, the grade II listed structure is still an essential part of the seafront's appeal. This view from 1911 shows the steamer *La Marguerite* sailing from the pier.

Lest we forget. The cenotaph was unveiled in 1922 to commemorate the 219 local servicemen who fell in the Great War. Subsequent panels were erected on the memorial commemorating those who gave their lives in the Second World War, as well as Lance Bombadier Llywelyn Evans, who served during the Iraq conflict in 2003. This Remembrance Day scene was taken around 1960.

The promenade cenotaph was not the first obelisk to mark Llandudno's fallen heroes. This monument to the fallen of the Boer War in South Africa was erected on the Great Orme.

The RNLI lifeboat station on Lloyd Street is often thought to be one of the strangest places to build a boathouse. However, when it was built in the 1860s the station was required to be equal in distance to both local shores and the train station. As this picture suggests the current lifeboat has outgrown its Lloyd Street home and moves are afoot to build a new station on the promenade. The Llandudno boat *Andy Pearce* is still the only lifeboat in the UK to have to be pulled through the streets to reach the shoreline.

The Town Hall on Lloyd Street is one of the finest buildings in Llandudno. The site was given by Lord Mostyn to commemorate Queen Victoria's Diamond Jubilee in 1897 and the building opened in 1902. The fact that the stylish development was built at twice its expected construction cost prompted a government inquiry at the time.

The Palladium on Gloddaeth Street is one of the most architecturally appealing buildings found in the centre of town. The Palladium cinema occupied this building from 1920 and it was once a popular venue for a night at the flicks. Sadly, time moved on even for this great picture house and dwindling audiences eventually forced its closure. The building is now a public house.

Bodlondeb Castle, Llandudno

One of the more eye-catching houses in the town is Bodlondeb Castle on Church Walks. During its colourful history the house has been used as a military hospital, hotel and school. When known as the Sywell House Hotel it prepared boys for public schools and the Royal Navy.

ON THIS VERY SHORE
DURING HAPPY RAMBLES WITH
LITTLE ALICE LIDDELL.
LEWIS CARROLL
WAS INSPIRED TO WRITE THAT
LITERARY TREASURE
'ALICE IN WONDERLAND'
WHICH HAS CHARMED CHILDREN
FOR GENERATIONS

UNVEILED BY
THE RT. HON. D. LLOYD GEORGE O.M. M.P.
SEPT. 6TH 1933.

There is scant evidence that Lewis Carroll actually visited the Liddell family in Pen Morfa (West Shore) yet this place is said to have inspired him to write his famous book *Alice's Adventures in Wonderland*. This famous memorial stands on the shoreline in recognition of the literary connection.

One of the more stylish buildings in the Llandudno area was the Lady Forester Convalescent Home at Craig-y-Don. It was opened in 1902 in memory of her late husband, General George Cecil Forester, the 3rd Baron of Forester and MP for Wenlock. The beautiful home provided free accommodation to poor convalescents and was very popular. It still stands today but since 1979 has accommodated the North Wales Medical Centre.

In 1925 Llandudno was fortunate to have been gifted this magnificent house at Fferm Bach Road in Craig-y-Don. The house and its unique collection of art, curios and relics had been bequeathed on the death of Francis Chandon as the new Rapallo House Museum. Its collection of exhibits was later moved and now forms an important part of the present Llandudno Museum on Gloddaeth Street.

eight

Making the news

One of Australia's most celebrated political figures spent much of his childhood in Llandudno. William 'Billy' Hughes lived at Abbey Road and spent seven years as a pupil at the Grammar School. Hughes was Australian Prime Minister from 1915 until 1923. In later years Billy Hughes returned to Llandudno to show his wife around his boyhood haunts and was given a rousing civic reception. Hughes once said of the town, 'I have always thought and contended; in spite of the claims of those watering places in various parts of the Empire and world that challenged its pre-eminence, that Llandudno is incomparably the most beautiful resort I have ever seen'. He died in 1952 with his fifty-eight years as an MP still a record in Australia.

It is questionable whether any holidaymaker has generated quite the impact as did Queen Elizabeth of Roumania in 1890. The consort to King Carol I had been staying in London, suffering bouts of depression, and visited the town in pursuit of rest and recuperation. However, from the moment the German-born Queen arrived on her five-week stay, huge crowds, sometimes numbered in their thousands, followed her every move as she journeyed about town. Shops she perused in Mostyn Street even boastfully displayed signs proclaiming 'By Royal Appointment'.

In May 1904 the Wild West Show of world-famous frontiersman Buffalo Bill came to town for a one-night performance at the Commissioners Field on Conwy Road. The two performances that day were priced at 1, 2, 4s per ticket and for 5s you could hire a box. William F. Cody, Buffalo Bill's real name, stirred considerable excitement in Llandudno. He was an authentic Pony Express rider, American Civil War soldier, Buffalo hunter and Indian fighter and his swashbuckling Wild West Show easily caught the public's imagination. Buffalo Bill always looked resplendent in his fringed buckskins and silver spurs and he remains one of the most distinguished performers ever to have appeared at Llandudno.

The inaugural journey of the first public tramcar, pictured here at Mostyn Street in 1907. Trams were an immediate success on the streets of Llandudno with almost 4,500 people using them on their first day of service.

Opposite above: The Odeon nurtured the career of many aspiring entertainers, few of whom went on to achieve their dreams of regular stage entertainment. This group were finalists in the 1939 North Wales Talent Competition, an event always guaranteed to attract a full house to the Odeon. The best known act to perform at the Odeon were four fresh-faced 'mop-topped' young men called The Beatles. They performed here on six consecutive nights in 1963.

Opposite below: Pictured in 1938 alongside the magnificent Christie Organ is nineteen-year-old Jess Yates. The Odeon organist went on to become one of Britain's top cinema organists, making over 1,000 live performances at forty-eight venues. He is reputed to have been the last of the great touring cinema organists, before moving on to develop an amazing show-business career with the BBC – as a designer, television presenter, writer, producer and director. Jess Yates continued hitting the headlines in the 1950s, '60s and '70s, becoming one of Britain's best loved television entertainers, with such hugely popular shows as *Picture Parade* and *Stars on Sunday.* At one point his Yorkshire television programme averaged 17 million viewers a week and the top stars of the day appeared on his shows. Jess Yates always retained strong links with the Llandudno area and for many years was owner of the Deganwy Castle Hotel.

Important royal occasions have always been marked by festivities at Llandudno. This rare faded image from 1936 shows the town's civic procession in memory of the late King George V. As with most important occasions, the Llandudno Town Band leads the procession.

Llandudno made a considerable commitment to supporting the war effort. In 1941 the town embarked on a mammoth effort to raise £137,000 to adopt a warship to be named HMS *Llandudno*. Many fundraising activities were undertaken for 'Warship Week' the culmination of which was this parade through town. The army and Llandudno Town Band can be seen here passing the National Westminster Bank on Mostyn Street.

Three years later and another important national savings campaign gets underway. A 'Salute the Soldier' procession is seen passing along the North Parade in 1944. Thousands of local people together with locally based service personnel participated in the celebration.

In 1977 the paddle steamer *Waverley* made a rare appearance in North Wales marking the centenary of Llandudno Pier. The world's last seagoing paddle steamer is preserved by the Paddle Steamer Preservation Society and is reputed by her owners to be the most photographed boat in the world. She returned in 2001, once more offering that wonderful sight of a steamer disembarking passengers at Llandudno.

Other local titles published by Tempus

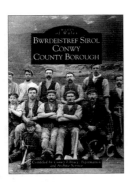

Conwy County Borough

CONWY LIBRARY, INFORMATION AND ARCHIVE SERVICE

This fascinating book is the first photographic record of the many communities that came together to create Conwy County Borough in 1996. Presenting around 200 images spanning 130 years of the County Borough's history, it shows something of the diversity of people's lives, both socially and at work in the traditional agricultural and quarrying industries. It also documents the meteoric rise of tourism that was to transform the area so completely.

0 7524 1121 7

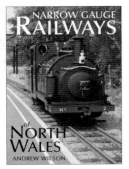

Narrow Gauge Railways of North Wales

ANDREW WILSON

One of the joys of the Welsh narrow gauge is its sheer variety and apparent antiquity. While many of the railways were designed from the outset and miniature mainlines, others were constructed on a shoestring. Illustrated with over 200 photographs, Andrew Wilson takes the reader on a nostalgic journey through North Wales, revisiting the rich diversity and charm of the Welsh narrow gauge railways and showing how they have changed in the last half century.

0 7524 2788 1

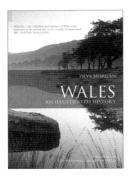

Wales, An Illustrated History

PRYS MORGAN

Wales was at the heart of the Industrial Revolution, with towns like Merthyr Tydfil driving the engine of the British Empire. The cultural and social divide between modern, industrialised Wales and the traditional agricultural areas is explored within this comprehensive volume.

0 7524 2970 1

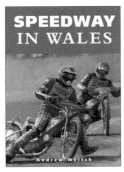

Speedway in Wales

ANDREW WELTCH

Speedway arrived in Wales at the end of 1928, the year the sport was introduced to Britain from Australia. Dirt-track racing was an immediate success, and thousands flocked to tracks in Cardiff, Pontypridd, Tredegar and Caerphilly over the following years. This book tells the fascinating boom-and-bust (and boom again) story of Welsh speedway, from the pioneer years, when the Cardiff-based Wales team seemed invincible, to the present day.

0 7524 2701 6

If you are interested in purchasing other books published by Tempus, or in case you have difficulty finding any Tempus books in your local bookshop, you can also place orders directly through our website

www.tempus-publishing.com